August brings the sheaves of corn,
When that harvest home is borne.

Warm September brings the fruit,
Sportsmen then begin to shoot.

Fresh October brings the pheasant,
Then to gather nuts is pleasant.

Dull November brings the blast,
Then the leaves are whirling fast.

Chill December brings the sleet,
Blazing fire and Christmas heat.

    Sara Coleridge

A Year of POEMS

*Illustrations by
Anne Grahame Johnstone*

DEAN

JANUARY

Flowers first, then petals fall,
Until there's not one left at all.

Then day by day, the berries grow,
Until the hedgerows burn and glow.

There are hips and haws —
 like bright red beads,

And inside, warm and safe,
 lie seeds.

BBC/Carole Ward

FEBRUARY

White Fields

In the winter time we go
Walking in the fields of snow;

Where there is no grass at all;
Where the top of every wall,

Every fence, and every tree
Is as white as white can be.

Pointing out the way we came –
Every one of them the same –

All across the fields there be
Prints in silver filigree;

And our mothers always know,
By the footprints in the snow,

Where it is the children go.

James Stephens

MARCH

Pippa's Song

The year's at the spring,
And day's at the morn;
Morning's at seven;
The hill-side's dew-pearled;
The lark's on the wing;
The snail's on the thorn;
God's in His heaven –
All's right with the world!

Robert Browning

APRIL

Wet

Wet wet wet
the world of melting winter,
icicles weeping themselves away
on the eaves
little brown rivers streaming
down the road
nibbling
at the edges of the tired snow,
    all puddled mud
    not a dry place to put
    a booted foot,
everything
    dripping
    slipping
    gushing
    slushing
and listen to that brook,
rushing
like a puppy loosed from its leash.

Lilian Moore

MAY

There is but one May in the year,
And sometimes May is wet and cold;
There is but one May in the year,
Before the year grows old.

Yet though it be the chilliest May,
With least of sun and most of showers,
Its wind and dew, its night and day,
Bring up the flowers.

Christina Rossetti

JUNE

In June

In June, haymaking, and heavy bees
Suddenly swarming on sagging branches;
Swifts dart, wheel about the hot sky,
Glide over pools, green with weed and
                                        dragonflies,
Sheep, streaming down from the hills
                                        to be shorn,
Cry all night to the thin wind;
Corn turns copper and gold in long fields,
                                        moon daisies
Whiter than midnight moths, tower over
                                        pimpernels,
Waiting to close red eyes at sundown;
Rain falls in a kind shower.
In June, all days are cherry ripe,
Sweeter than strawberries.

    Leonard Clark

JULY

A Boy's Song

Where the pools are bright and deep,
Where the grey trout lies asleep,
Up the river and o'er the lea –
That's the way for Billy and me.

Where the blackbird sings the latest,
Where the hawthorn blooms the sweetest,
Where the nestlings chirp and flee –
That's the way for Billy and me.

Where the mowers mow the cleanest,
Where the hay lies thick and greenest,
There to trace the homeward bee –
That's the way for Billy and me.

There let us walk, there let us play,
Through the meadow among the hay,
Up the water and over the lea –
That's the way for Billy and me.

James Hogg

AUGUST

August Afternoon

Where shall we go?
    What shall we play?
What shall we do
    On a hot summer day?

We'll sit in the swing.
    Go low. Go high.
And drink lemonade
    Till the glass is dry.

One straw for you,
    One straw for me,
In the cool green shade
    Of the walnut tree.

*Marion Edey
and Dorothy Grider*

SEPTEMBER

Autumn

Yellow the bracken
Golden the sheaves,
Rosy the apples,
Crimson the leaves;

Mist on the hillside;
Clouds grey and white.
Autumn,
   good morning!
Summer,
   good night!

Florence Hoatson

OCTOBER

Go Wind

Go wind, blow
Push wind, swoosh.
   Shake things
   take things
   make things
     fly.

   Ring things
   swing things
   fling things
     high.

Go wind, blow
Push things . . . wheee.
   No, wind, no.
   Not me —
   not *me*.

Lilian Moore

NOVEMBER

Wood for Burning

Beechwood fires burn bright and clear
If the logs are kept a year;
Chestnut's only good they say
If for years 'tis stored away;
Birch and firwood burn too fast,
Blaze too bright and do not last;
But ashwood green and ashwood brown
Are fit for a Queen with a golden crown.

Oaken logs if dry and old
Keep away the winter's cold;
Poplar gives a bitter smoke,
Fills your eyes and makes you choke;
Elmwood burns like churchyard mould,
Even the very flames are cold;
Applewood will scent the room,
Pearwood smells like flowers in bloom;
But ashwood wet and ashwood dry,
A King may warm his slippers by.

Traditional

DECEMBER

The holly and the ivy,
When they are both full grown,
Of all the trees that are in the wood,
The holly bears the crown.

> *The rising of the sun*
> *And the running of the deer,*
> *The playing of the merry organ,*
> *Sweet singing in the choir.*

The holly bears a blossom,
As white as the lily flower,
And Mary bore sweet Jesus Christ,
To be our sweet Saviour.

The holly bears a berry,
As red as any blood,
And Mary bore sweet Jesus Christ,
To do poor sinners good.

The holly bears a prickle,
As sharp as any thorn,
And Mary bore sweet Jesus Christ,
On Christmas Day in the morn.

Traditional

GOOD MORNING
WHEN IT'S MORNING

Good morning when it's morning
Good night when it is night
Good evening when it's dark out
Good day when it is light
Good morning to the sunshine
Good evening to the sky
And when it's time to go away
Good-bye
Good-bye
Good-bye.

Mary Ann Hoberman